PIANO • VOCAL • GUITAR

2ND EDITION

BROADWAY JAZZ

ISBN-13: 978-0-7935-1445-8
ISBN-10: 0-7935-1445-2

HAL•LEONARD® CORPORATION

7777 W. BLUEMOUND RD. P.O. BOX 13819 MILWAUKEE, WI 53213

For all works contained herein:
Unauthorized copying, arranging, adapting, recording or public performance is an infringement of copyright.
Infringers are liable under the law.

Visit Hal Leonard Online at
www.halleonard.com

BROADWAY

JAZZ

AIN'T MISBEHAVIN'
from AIN'T MISBEHAVIN'

Words by ANDY RAZAF
Music by THOMAS "FATS" WALLER
and HARRY BROOKS

Boy: Though it's a fick - le
Girl: Your type of man is

age
rare,

With flirt - ing all the rage,
I know you real - ly care,

Copyright © 1929 by Mills Music, Inc.
Copyright Renewed, Assigned to Mills Music, Inc., Chappell & Co. and Razaf Music Co. in the United States
All Rights for Razaf Music Co. Administered by The Songwriters Guild Of America
International Copyright Secured   All Rights Reserved

CAN'T HELP LOVIN' DAT MAN

from SHOW BOAT

Lyrics by OSCAR HAMMERSTEIN II
Music by JEROME KERN

Oh lis-ten, sis-ter, I love my Mis-ter man _____ and I can't _____ tell yo' why. _____ Dere ain't no rea-son why I should love dat man. _____ it must be sump-in' dat _____

Copyright © 1927 UNIVERSAL - POLYGRAM INTERNATIONAL PUBLISHING, INC.
Copyright Renewed
All Rights Reserved   Used by Permission

ALL THE THINGS YOU ARE

from VERY WARM FOR MAY

Lyrics by OSCAR HAMMERSTEIN II
Music by JEROME KERN

Copyright © 1939 UNIVERSAL - POLYGRAM INTERNATIONAL PUBLISHING, INC.
Copyright Renewed
All Rights Reserved   Used by Permission

BEWITCHED
from PAL JOEY

Words by LORENZ HART
Music by RICHARD RODGERS

He's a fool and don't I know it, But a fool can have his charms;

I'm in love and don't I show it, Like a babe in arms.

Love's the same old sad sen - sa - tion, Late - ly I've not slept a wink,

Copyright © 1941 (Renewed) by Chappell & Co.
Rights for the Extended Renewal Term in the U.S. Controlled by Williamson Music and WB Music Corp. o/b/o The Estate of Lorenz Hart
International Copyright Secured   All Rights Reserved

21

COME RAIN OR COME SHINE
from ST. LOUIS WOMAN

Words by JOHNNY MERCER
Music by HAROLD ARLEN

Copyright © 1946 (Renewed) by Chappell & Co. and S.A. Music Co.
International Copyright Secured   All Rights Reserved

HONEYSUCKLE ROSE
from AIN'T MISBEHAVIN'

Words by ANDY RAZAF
Music by THOMAS "FATS" WALLER

Copyright © 1929 by Chappell & Co. and Razaf Music Co. in the United States
Copyright Renewed
All Rights for Razaf Music Co. Administered by The Songwriters Guild Of America
International Copyright Secured   All Rights Reserved

FROM THIS MOMENT ON

from OUT OF THIS WORLD

Words and Music by
COLE PORTER

Moderately slow

Now that we are close, no more nights mor-ose, Now that we are one, the be-guine has just be-gun. Now that we're side by side,

Copyright © 1950 by Cole Porter
Copyright Renewed, Assigned to Robert H. Montgomery, Trustee of the Cole Porter Musical and Literary Property Trusts
Chappell & Co. owner of publication and allied rights throughout the world
International Copyright Secured   All Rights Reserved

the fu- ture looks so gay, Now we are al- i- bied when we

Suddenly lively

say: _____

Refrain *(lively, but not rushed)*

From this mo- ment on, _____

you for me, dear,

HAVE YOU MET MISS JONES?

from I'D RATHER BE RIGHT

Words by LORENZ HART
Music by RICHARD RODGERS

Copyright © 1937 (Renewed) by Chappell & Co.
Rights for the Extended Renewal Term in the U.S. Controlled by Williamson Music and WB Music Corp. o/b/o The Estate Of Lorenz Hart
International Copyright Secured   All Rights Reserved

HOW HIGH THE MOON

from TWO FOR THE SHOW

Words by NANCY HAMILTON
Music by MORGAN LEWIS

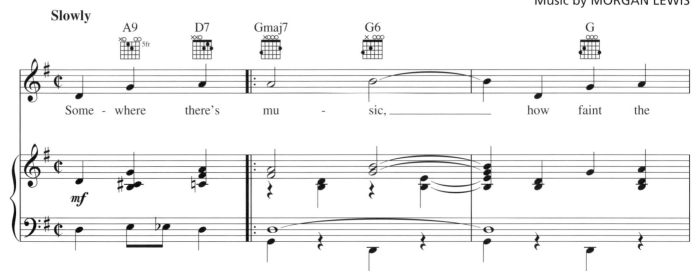

Some - where there's mu - sic, _____ how faint the

tune! _____ Some - where there's heav - en, _____

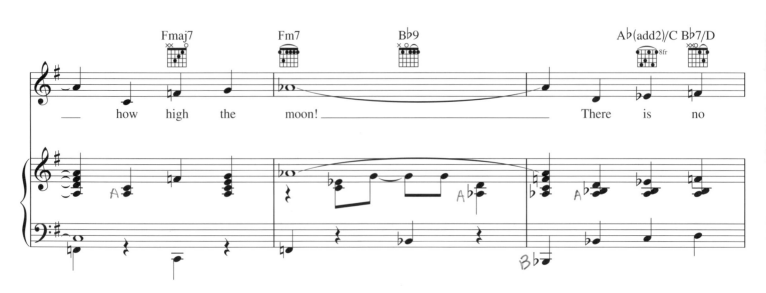

___ how high the moon! _____ There is no

Copyright © 1940 by Chappell & Co.
Copyright Renewed
International Copyright Secured   All Rights Reserved

IF I WERE A BELL

from GUYS AND DOLLS

By FRANK LOESSER

© 1950 (Renewed) FRANK MUSIC CORP.
All Rights Reserved

I COULD WRITE A BOOK

from PAL JOEY

Words by LORENZ HART
Music by RICHARD RODGERS

Copyright © 1940 (Renewed) by Chappell & Co.
Rights for the Extended Renewal Term in the U.S. Controlled by Williamson Music and WB Music Corp. o/b/o The Estate Of Lorenz Hart
International Copyright Secured   All Rights Reserved

I DIDN'T KNOW WHAT TIME IT WAS

from TOO MANY GIRLS

Words by LORENZ HART
Music by RICHARD RODGERS

Copyright © 1939 (Renewed) by Chappell & Co.
Rights for the Extended Renewal Term in the U.S. Controlled by Williamson Music and WB Music Corp. o/b/o The Estate Of Lorenz Hart
International Copyright Secured   All Rights Reserved

I LOVE PARIS
from CAN-CAN

Words and Music by
COLE PORTER

Copyright © 1953 by Cole Porter
Copyright Renewed, Assigned to Robert H. Montgomery, Trustee of the Cole Porter Musical and Literary Property Trusts
Chappell & Co. owner of publication and allied rights throughout the world
International Copyright Secured   All Rights Reserved

I'VE NEVER BEEN IN LOVE BEFORE

from GUYS AND DOLLS

By FRANK LOESSER

© 1950 (Renewed) FRANK MUSIC CORP.
All Rights Reserved

IT MIGHT AS WELL BE SPRING

from STATE FAIR

Lyrics by OSCAR HAMMERSTEIN II
Music by RICHARD RODGERS

Moderately

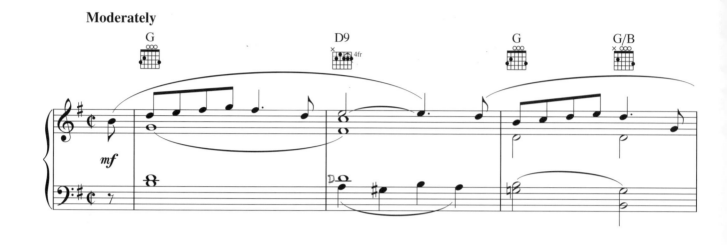

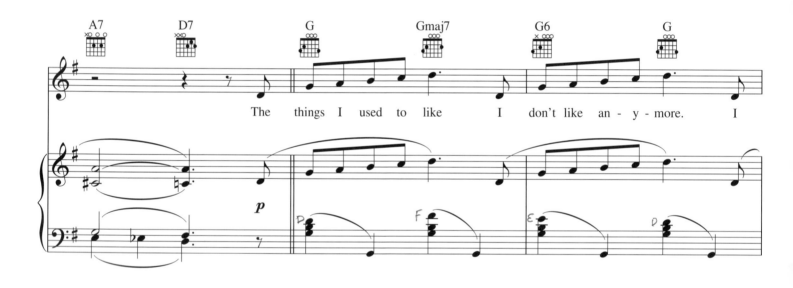

The things I used to like I don't like an-y-more. I

want a lot of oth-er things I've nev-er had be-fore. It's just like moth-er

Copyright © 1945 by WILLIAMSON MUSIC
Copyright Renewed
International Copyright Secured All Rights Reserved

IT'S ALL RIGHT WITH ME

from CAN-CAN

Words and Music by
COLE PORTER

Steadily moving Fox Trot

Copyright © 1953 by Cole Porter
Copyright Renewed, Assigned to Robert H. Montgomery, Trustee of the Cole Porter Musical and Literary Property Trusts
Chappell & Co. owner of publication and allied rights throughout the world
International Copyright Secured   All Rights Reserved

IT'S DE-LOVELY
from RED, HOT AND BLUE!

Words and Music by
COLE PORTER

Rhythmically

The night is young, the skies are clear and if you want to go

walk-ing, dear, it's de-light-ful, it's de-li-cious, it's de-love-ly.

I un-der-stand the rea-son why you're sen-ti-men-tal, 'cause

Copyright © 1936 by Chappell & Co.
Copyright Renewed, Assigned to Robert H. Montgomery, Trustee of the Cole Porter Musical and Literary Property Trusts
Chappell & Co. owner of publication and allied rights throughout the world
International Copyright Secured   All Rights Reserved

*Pronounced "delukes"

JUST IN TIME
from BELLS ARE RINGING

Words by BETTY COMDEN and ADOLPH GREEN
Music by JULE STYNE

Copyright © 1956 by Betty Comden, Adolph Green and Jule Styne
Copyright Renewed
Stratford Music Corporation, owner of publication and allied rights throughout the world
Chappell & Co., Administrator
International Copyright Secured   All Rights Reserved

THE LADY IS A TRAMP

from BABES IN ARMS

Words by LORENZ HART
Music by RICHARD RODGERS

Copyright © 1937 (Renewed) by Chappell & Co.
Rights for the Extended Renewal Term in the U.S. Controlled by Williamson Music and WB Music Corp. o/b/o The Estate Of Lorenz Hart
International Copyright Secured   All Rights Reserved

MOOD INDIGO
from SOPHISTICATED LADIES

Words and Music by DUKE ELLINGTON,
IRVING MILLS and ALBANY BIGARD

Copyright © 1931 (Renewed 1958) and Assigned to Famous Music LLC, EMI Mills Music Inc. and Indigo Mood Music c/o The Songwriters Guild Of America in the U.S.A.
Rights for the world outside the U.S.A. Controlled by EMI Mills Music Inc. (Publishing) and Warner Bros. Publications U.S. Inc. (Print)
International Copyright Secured   All Rights Reserved

MY FAVORITE THINGS
from THE SOUND OF MUSIC

Lyrics by OSCAR HAMMERSTEIN II
Music by RICHARD RODGERS

Copyright © 1959 by Richard Rodgers and Oscar Hammerstein II
Copyright Renewed
WILLIAMSON MUSIC owner of publication and allied rights throughout the world
International Copyright Secured   All Rights Reserved

MY FUNNY VALENTINE

from BABES IN ARMS

Words by LORENZ HART
Music by RICHARD RODGERS

Copyright © 1937 (Renewed) by Chappell & Co.
Rights for the Extended Renewal Term in the U.S. Controlled by Williamson Music and WB Music Corp. o/b/o The Estate Of Lorenz Hart
International Copyright Secured   All Rights Reserved

8vb ⌐

OLD DEVIL MOON

from FINIAN'S RAINBOW

Words by E.Y. "YIP" HARBURG
Music by BURTON LANE

Copyright © 1946 by Chappell & Co. and Glocca Morra Music
Copyright Renewed
All Rights for Glocca Morra Music Administered by Next Decade Entertainment, Inc.
International Copyright Secured   All Rights Reserved

ON A CLEAR DAY
(You Can See Forever)
from ON A CLEAR DAY YOU CAN SEE FOREVER

Words by ALAN JAY LERNER
Music by BURTON LANE

Copyright © 1965 by Chappell & Co. and WB Music Corp. in the United States
Copyright Renewed
Chappell & Co. owner of publication and allied rights for the rest of the world
International Copyright Secured   All Rights Reserved

THE OTHER SIDE OF THE TRACKS

from LITTLE ME

Music by CY COLEMAN
Lyrics by CAROLYN LEIGH

Copyright © 1962 Notable Music Company, Inc. and EMI Carwin Music Inc.
Copyright Renewed
All Rights for Notable Music Company, Inc. Administered by Chrysalis Music
All Rights Reserved   Used by Permission

SATIN DOLL
from SOPHISTICATED LADIES

Words by JOHNNY MERCER and BILLY STRAYHORN
Music by DUKE ELLINGTON

Copyright © 1958 (Renewed 1986) and Assigned to Famous Music LLC, WB Music Corp. and Tempo Music, Inc. c/o Music Sales Corporation in the U.S.A.
Rights for the world outside the U.S.A. Controlled by Tempo Music, Inc. c/o Music Sales Corporation
International Copyright Secured   All Rights Reserved

SMALL WORLD
from GYPSY

Words by STEPHEN SONDHEIM
Music by JULE STYNE

Copyright © 1959 by Stratford Music Corporation and Williamson Music, Inc.
Copyright Renewed
All Rights Administered by Chappell & Co.
International Copyright Secured   All Rights Reserved

SPEAK LOW

from the Musical Production ONE TOUCH OF VENUS

Words by OGDEN NASH
Music by KURT WEILL

TRO - © Copyright 1943 (Renewed) Hampshire House Publishing Corp., New York and Chappell & Co., Los Angeles, CA
International Copyright Secured
All Rights Reserved Including Public Performance For Profit
Used by Permission

THE SURREY WITH THE FRINGE ON TOP

from OKLAHOMA!

Lyrics by OSCAR HAMMERSTEIN II
Music by RICHARD RODGERS

Brightly

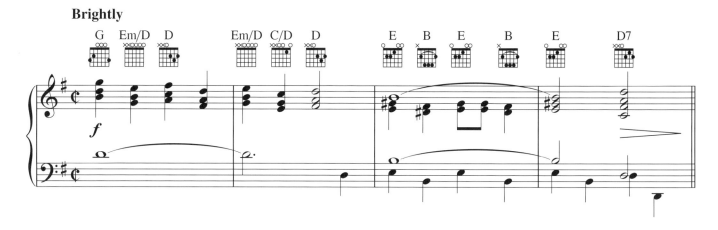

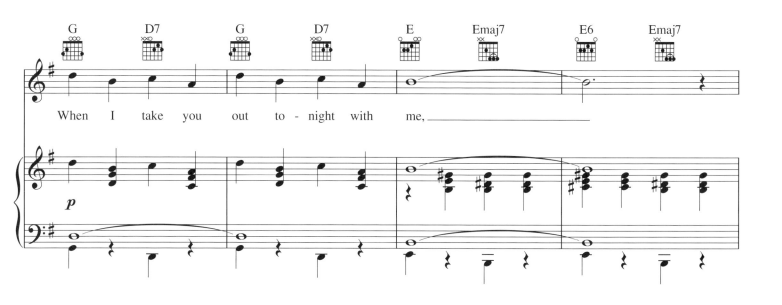

When I take you out to-night with me, _____

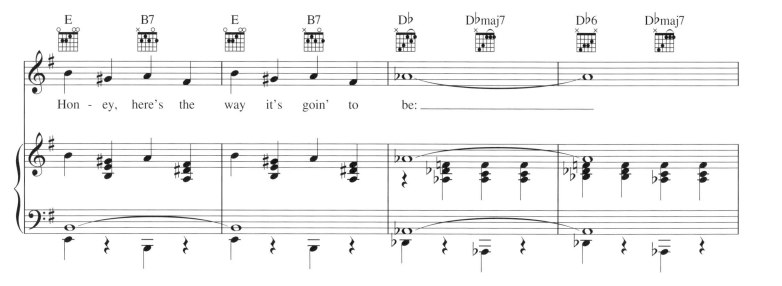

Hon- ey, here's the way it's goin' to be: _____

Copyright © 1943 by WILLIAMSON MUSIC
Copyright Renewed
International Copyright Secured   All Rights Reserved

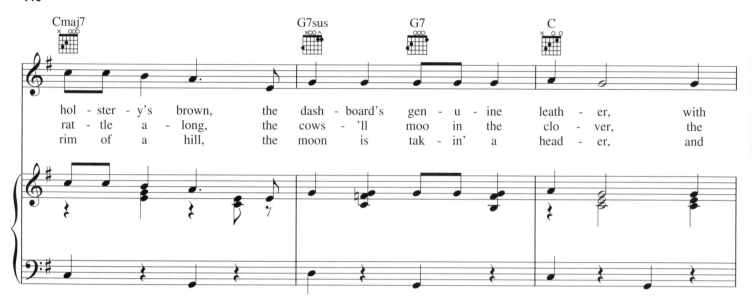

hol - ster - y's brown, the dash - board's gen - u - ine leath - er, with
rat - tle a - long, the cows - 'll moo in the clo - ver, with the
rim of a hill, the moon is tak - in' a head - er, and

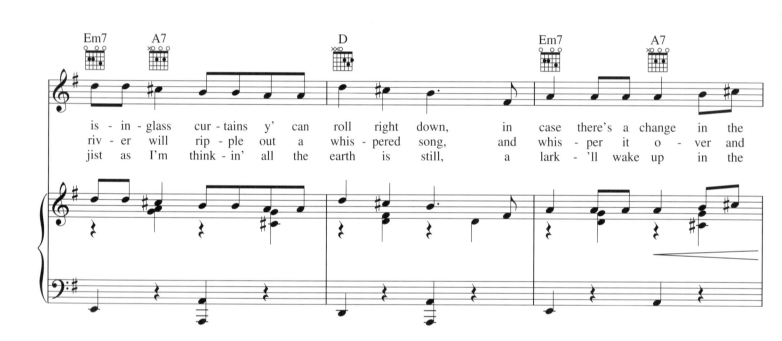

is - in - glass cur - tains y' can roll right down, in case there's a change in the
riv - er will rip - ple out a whis - pered song, and whis - per it o - ver and
jist as I'm think - in' all the earth is still, a lark - 'll wake up in the

weath - er.   Two bright side - lights's wink - in' and blink - in',   ain't no fin - er
o - ver: Don't you wisht y'd go on for - ev - er?   Don't you wisht y'd
med - der.   Hush, you bird, my ba - by's a - sleep - in'!   May - be got a

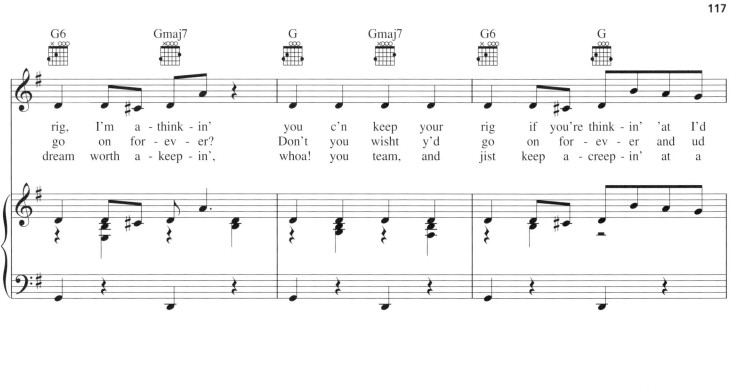

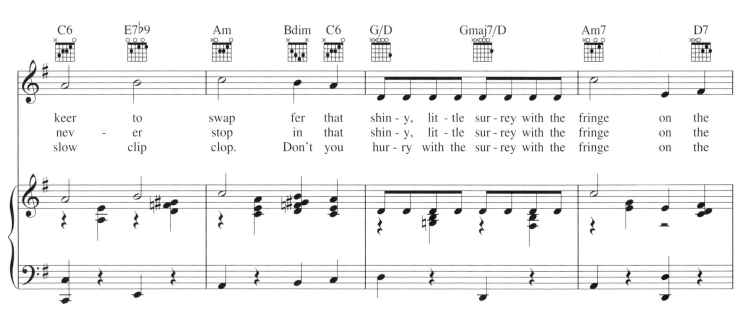

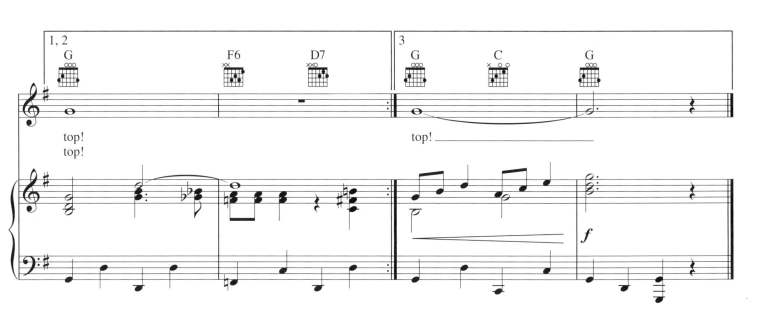

THERE'S A SMALL HOTEL
from ON YOUR TOES

Words by LORENZ HART
Music by RICHARD RODGERS

Copyright © 1936 (Renewed) by Chappell & Co.
Rights for the Extended Renewal Term in the U.S. Controlled by Williamson Music and WB Music Corp. o/b/o The Estate Of Lorenz Hart
International Copyright Secured   All Rights Reserved

THIS CAN'T BE LOVE

from THE BOYS FROM SYRACUSE

Words by LORENZ HART
Music by RICHARD RODGERS

Copyright © 1938 (Renewed) by Chappell & Co.
Rights for the Extended Renewal Term in the U.S. Controlled by Williamson Music and WB Music Corp. o/b/o The Estate Of Lorenz Hart
International Copyright Secured   All Rights Reserved

TOO CLOSE FOR COMFORT

from the Musical MR. WONDERFUL

Words and Music by JERRY BOCK,
LARRY HOLOFCENER and GEORGE WEISS

Copyright © 1956 by The Herald Square Music Co.
Copyright Renewed and Assigned to Range Road Music Inc., Quartet Music, Abilene Music, Inc. and Jerry Bock Enterprises
All Rights on behalf of Abilene Music, Inc. Administered by The Songwriters Guild of America
International Copyright Secured   All Rights Reserved
Used by Permission

WHERE OR WHEN

from BABES IN ARMS

Words by LORENZ HART
Music by RICHARD RODGERS

Copyright © 1937 (Renewed) by Chappell & Co.
Rights for the Extended Renewal Term in the U.S. Controlled by Williamson Music and WB Music Corp. o/b/o The Estate Of Lorenz Hart
International Copyright Secured   All Rights Reserved

The clothes you're wear-ing are the clothes you wore. The
smile you are smil-ing you were smil-ing then, but I can't re-mem-ber where or
when. Some things that hap-pen for the
first time, seem to be hap-pen-ing a-

WHO CAN I TURN TO
(When Nobody Needs Me)
from THE ROAR OF THE GREASEPAINT – THE SMELL OF THE CROWD

Words and Music by LESLIE BRICUSSE
and ANTHONY NEWLEY

Slowly, with expression

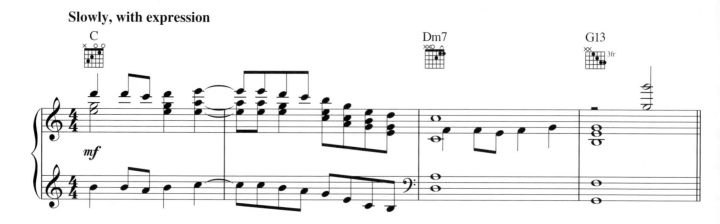

Who can I turn to _____ when no-bod-y needs me? _____ My

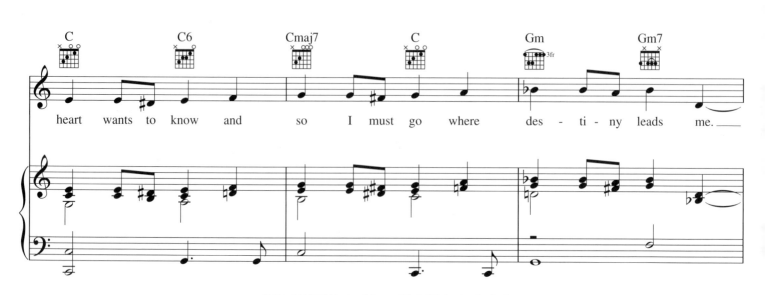

heart wants to know and so I must go where des-ti-ny leads me.

© Copyright 1964 (Renewed) Concord Music Ltd., London, England
TRO - Musical Comedy Productions, Inc., New York, controls all publication rights for the U.S.A. and Canada
International Copyright Secured
All Rights Reserved Including Public Performance For Profit
Used by Permission

YOU BETTER GO NOW

from NEW FACES OF 1936

Words by BICKLEY REICHNER
Music by ROBERT GRAHAM

Copyright © 1936 by Chappell & Co.
Copyright Renewed
International Copyright Secured   All Rights Reserved

YESTERDAYS

from ROBERTA

Words by OTTO HARBACH
Music by JEROME KERN

Yes - ter - days, yes - ter - days, days I knew as
youth was mine, truth was mine, joy - ous, free and

hap - py, sweet se - ques - tered days.
flam - ing life, for - sooth, was mine.

Copyright © 1933 UNIVERSAL - POLYGRAM INTERNATIONAL PUBLISHING, INC.
Copyright Renewed
All Rights Reserved   Used by Permission

YOU'RE THE CREAM IN MY COFFEE

from HOLD EVERYTHING

Words and Music by B.G. DeSYLVA,
LEW BROWN and RAY HENDERSON

Copyright © 1928 by Chappell & Co., Stephen Ballentine Music Publishing Co. and Ray Henderson Music
Copyright Renewed
International Copyright Secured   All Rights Reserved